baby
sign language
basics

HAY HOUSE TITLES OF RELATED INTEREST

Books

The Crystal Children: *A Guide to the Newest Generation of Psychic and Sensitive Children,* by Doreen Virtue, Ph.D.

Practical Parenting, by Montel Williams and Jeffrey Gardère, Ph.D.

Seven Secrets to Raising a Happy and Healthy Child: *The Ayurvedic Approach to Parenting,* by Joyce Golden Seyburn

Card Decks

Rainy-Day Fun: *Easy Indoor Games and Activities Your Kids Will Love,* from the Publishers of *Parenting* magazine

Sign Language for Babies: *50 Easy Words to Learn—From Sleep to I Love You,* from the Publishers of *Parenting* magazine

baby sign language basics

Early Communication for Hearing Babies and Toddlers

Monta Z. Briant

HAY HOUSE, INC.
Carlsbad, California
London • Sydney • Johannesburg
Vancouver • Hong Kong

Published and distributed in the United States by: Hay House, Inc., P.O. Box 5100, Carlsbad, CA 92018-5100 • *Phone:* (760) 431-7695 or (800) 654-5126 • *Fax:* (760) 431-6948 or (800) 650-5115 • www.hayhouse.com • *Published and distributed in Australia by:* Hay House Australia, Ltd., 18/36 Ralph St., Alexandria NSW 2015 • *Phone:* 612-9669-4299 • *Fax:* 612-9669-4144 • www.hayhouse.com.au • *Published and distributed in the United Kingdom by:* Hay House UK, Ltd. • Unit 62, Canalot Studios • 222 Kensal Rd., London W10 5BN • *Phone:* 44-20-8962-1230 • *Fax:* 44-20-8962-1239 • www.hayhouse.co.uk • *Published and distributed in the Republic of South Africa by:* Hay House SA (Pty), Ltd., P.O. Box 990, Witkoppen 2068 • *Phone/Fax:* 2711-7012233 • orders@psdprom.co.za • *Distributed in Canada by:* Raincoast • 9050 Shaughnessy St., Vancouver, B.C. V6P 6E5 • *Phone:* (604) 323-7100 • *Fax:* (604) 323-2600

Editorial supervision: Jill Kramer   *Design and illustrations:* Summer McStravick
Interior photos: Gregory Bertolini

ISBN 1-4019-0290-1

07 06 05 04   5 4 3 2
1st printing, February 2004
2nd printing, February 2004
Printed in Canada

✖ ✖ ✖

For my own signing baby, Sirena, and for my loving husband, Paul. I certainly could not have done any of this without both of you!

✖ ✖ ✖

contents

PART II: GETTING STARTED

PART III: NOW YOU'RE SIGNING!

preface

When I was pregnant with my daughter, Sirena, my mother attended a baby sign language class through her local community college. I thought it was pretty funny that my mom was taking a parenting class 34 years after she had me, but I was also intrigued by the idea of being able to communicate with my baby before she could talk—what would she say? There was no such class in my community at the time, so I was excited to hear what my mom had learned when she next came to visit me in San Diego.

Little could I have known that signing with Sirena would be the most amazing experience for my husband and me, to the point that we don't know what we would have done without it! Of course, signing with our baby reduced frustration by taking a lot of the guesswork out of parenting and helped us meet Sirena's needs more easily, but there was so much more. The best part was getting to know our baby on a level that wouldn't have been possible otherwise. And once Sirena began signing back, I became a "baby sign-language evangelist," chasing down anyone I saw with a baby to tell them about signing with babies: in the supermarket checkout line, on walks, and at the playground. I wanted to share this incredible gift with every new parent.

I've since found a more efficient means of spreading the good news than accosting anyone pushing a stroller. In order to stay at home with Sirena, I decided to teach baby sign language classes. My company, Baby Sign Language Workshops, offers parent/teacher-focused workshops and parent/

child-signing classes throughout San Diego County.

This book will start you and your baby on an amazing journey of communication and discovery—a discovery of each other *and* a discovery of your new world together.

Your baby is trying to tell you something . . . so don't wait to communicate!

acknowledgments

I'd like to thank Drs. Linda Acredolo and Susan Goodwyn for their pioneering research in the field of baby sign language. I'd also like to thank Mr. Joseph Garcia and the entire staff of Sign2Me/Northlight Communications for all their incredible support and encouragement in getting my classes up and running, and Drs. Michelle Anthony and Reyna Lindhert for their wonderfully designed curriculum and teaching materials and personal encouragement. Last but not least, I want to thank all the members of the Sign with Your Baby Presenters' Network for sharing ideas, encouragement, and support. Together we're making baby sign language available to everyone who has contact with a preverbal child.

introduction

As a new or prospective parent, you may be thinking that signing with your baby sounds pretty neat, but you're also probably thinking that you'll be pretty busy with a new baby, so learning sign language won't be at the top of your list of priorities when the dirty diapers and strained peas start to fly.

Let me assure you that signing with your baby is easy—it's certainly much easier than *not* signing with your baby! Although we call it "baby sign language" and the signs we recommend using are actual American Sign Language (ASL) signs, you don't need to become fluent in ASL to communicate with your baby. Think of the book you now hold in your hands as the "baby talk" version of signing, and if a six-month-old baby can learn to do this, so can you.

Baby Sign Language Basics includes everything you need to get started right now. Along with 60 of the most useful signs (which are located in the Appendix), you'll find developmental information, strategies for getting your baby's attention, and engaging play-time signing activities and songs. When using this book, watch for words highlighted in **BOLD CAPS,** as they represent signed words.

This book is small enough for the diaper bag, so don't leave home without it!

[**Author's Note:** In order to avoid the awkward *he/she* con-struction, I've opted to alternate the use of the masculine and feminine pronouns throughout this book. Please note that the same information applies universally to both girls and boys.]

part 1

about baby
sign language

chapter 1

Baby Sign Language
Saves the Day,
Keeping Elephants at Bay

My then-ten-month-old daughter, Sirena, had always been easy to put to bed, so when she clung to me and cried one warm night, I wondered what could be wrong. Was she suddenly old enough to protest bedtime?

I looked at her and asked, "What's wrong?" simultaneously shrugging my shoulders and lifting my hands, palms up, in the natural gesture that is also the American Sign Language (ASL) sign for **WHAT?**

My tiny daughter immediately pointed to the open window and waved one hand in an arc out from her face, a gesture that I recognized as her approximation of the ASL sign for **ELEPHANT.** Now, I already knew that Sirena was terrified of elephants, expressing

4

this when she saw them at the zoo and on video—even a cute, fluffy hand puppet wasn't okay.

I'd also noticed that recently Sirena had begun signing **ELEPHANT** whenever she heard a car alarm or siren, which she'd apparently decided were noises made by elephants, so I followed her gaze to the window that, until this evening, had been closed while she slept. Suddenly I saw my urban neighborhood through my baby's eyes: a noisy place full of trumpeting elephants who were out of sight yet clearly around each corner, just waiting to reach or climb through a window carelessly left open!

I closed and locked the window and shut the blinds, and my sweet little girl went happily to sleep.

For the first time it really hit me just how valuable baby sign language was. If Sirena hadn't been able to communicate her specific fear through signing, I might have, in my ignorance, left her alone, crying in her crib, terrified of the car-alarm "elephants" outside.

chapter 2

What Is
Baby Sign Language?

Baby sign language is the practice of using symbolic gestures to enhance your verbal interactions with your baby. Using symbolic gestures is something all human beings do naturally—for example, when your baby lifts her arms to be picked up or points at something to draw your attention to it.

Not only is it completely natural to use symbolic gestures, it's nearly impossible to stop yourself from doing it—I mean, imagine trying to give directions to someone without using your hands! You'd probably have to sit on them to keep from gesturing, and you'd very likely find your head or entire body jerking or leaning in the direction of what you described (for example, "Turn left at the Shell station and turn right at the 7-11"). By the same token, if you use particular gestures to enhance certain words when you interact with your baby, she'll learn to use the same gestures you do, so communication will come along a lot better.

In this book, we'll use ASL signs as our symbolic gestures. While it *is* possible to use "made-up" signs, I feel that ASL signs are preferable for a number of reasons. First of all, if you're going to take the time to teach your baby something, why not teach something that she can use for a lifetime, rather than something that will just be discarded as soon as she learns to talk? At age two, Sirena was already able to use her signs to communicate with a deaf mother and her hearing/signing child, as well as with a Down's syndrome adult who used some signing.

Another good reason to stick with ASL is all the wonderful teaching resources that are available. Once your baby starts signing in earnest, she'll start asking you for signs for everything, so you're going to need more than the 60 signs contained in this book. At your local library, you can pick up an ASL dictionary containing thousands of signs, along with ASL children's books, which not only allow your child to see the sign on the page, but also serve as a parent's "cheat sheet" as you read and sign the story to your child.

Last, but certainly not least, ASL is being used with increasing frequency in child-care and preschool programs. Signing in infant and toddler programs cuts down on aggressive behavior, including hitting and biting; it works wonderfully as a "language bridge" between children who speak different languages; and it helps to include special-needs children with their peers. Imagine seeing your child signing with her deaf and hard-of-hearing friends! There are so many benefits on so many levels here. Speaking of which, the next chapter explains these benefits in detail.

chapter 3

The Benefits

During their long-term research study that was funded by the National Institutes of Health, Drs. Linda Acredolo and Susan Goodwyn found that signing with hearing babies had many short *and* long-term advantages. More than 140 families participating in the study were randomly assigned to either a signing or nonsigning (control) group. The groups were equal with respect to family education/income level and the children's gender, birth order, and tendency to vocalize or verbalize words. They found that the signing group enjoyed the following benefits:

1. Signing empowers babies to communicate very early in life. Signing empowers babies to communicate *specific* things, such as fears or location of pain. Even more amazing, signing allows babies to bring up topics of conversation that interest them—something no amount of crying can do!

2. Signing increases self-esteem. Signing allows babies to begin participating as contributing members of the household early on. You'll be absolutely thrilled when your baby shares his thoughts with you, and your *baby* will be thrilled that you understand and value what he has to say. Signing gives your baby a measure of self-sufficiency early on by allowing him a way to communicate his needs, feelings, and observations.

3. Signing reduces frustration for parents and babies alike. Babies who sign experience less frustration, crying, and tantrums. It isn't hard to see why. Imagine not being able to communicate even your most basic needs to the only person who could provide for them—you'd cry, too!

4. Signing enhances language skills. Signing babies tend to talk earlier and build vocabulary faster than their nonsigning peers. On average, children who signed as babies have 50 more spoken words in their vocabularies by age two than children who didn't sign. (That's not even counting all the *signed* words they're using by then!)

5. Signing enhances bonding and enriches parent/child interactions. You'll naturally have a richer and closer relationship with your baby when you have two-way communication. Signing also enables you to be a more compassionate caregiver—since you can understand your baby's specific fears and concerns, this will help build a foundation of trust between you and your baby.

6. Signing gives a window into your child's mind and personality. For the parent, this is the best benefit, as far as I'm concerned—it's a parent's reward for signing with their baby. I can't adequately describe the wonder you'll feel as your baby begins to share his fresh interpretation of the world with you.

Your baby misses nothing, and will show you things that you've walked past 1,000 times without seeing. We adults are so rushed most of the time that we walk through this beautiful world with tunnel vision. Signing with your baby will force you to slow down once in a while and look at the world through his eyes—you'll find that it's a bright, new, wonderful place full of amazing things to see and explore. Only by signing with your baby will you get such an early glimpse into your child's world.

7. Signing allows you to see just how smart your baby really is. Oftentimes, parents under-estimate how much their very young child is capable of understanding. By the time Sirena was 15 months old, I was talking to her about pretty much anything that I didn't think would scare her, and her questions and level of reasoning amazed me on a daily basis.

One week, Sirena and I made two visits to the home of a pregnant neighbor. I tried to explain to my then 15-month-old daughter about the baby in our neighbor's tummy and how when it came, our neighbor would be a mommy. Sirena looked worried, and I hoped I hadn't traumatized her somehow. I wondered what she was thinking.

A few days later, after the baby had arrived, and Sirena and I walked down the block again to see the new mother and baby and to deliver a casserole. My daughter acted shy and again wore a worried little furrow in her brow. On the way home, as I tried to explain about the birth again, Sirena stopped me. "Mama," she said, and then signed **BABY CHICK** and the sign she used for **OPEN/TAKE OUT**.

I could scarcely believe my eyes. My 15-month-old was asking me if a baby coming out of the mommy's tummy was anything like a baby chick coming out of an egg. "Yes, you're right, honey!" I assured her. "They're both being born. A chick is born out of an egg, and babies are born out of their mommy's tummy."

The furrow in Sirena's brow instantly disappeared. She hadn't been worried at all—she'd been thinking very hard. It's amazing that she didn't have smoke coming out of her ears!

Imagine if Sirena had been forced to wait until she could actually *say* the words necessary to ask this question. How frustrating! And how unfortunate to miss such a perfect learning opportunity. Children learn most effectively when lessons are tied in with things that are already of interest to them, so signing allows them to ask questions about their interests and observations long before they can talk.

8. Signing increases IQ. As a follow-up to their study, Acredolo and Goodwyn tested the original participants' IQ when the children were eight years old. Their findings showed that the children who had signed as babies scored an average of 12 points higher than the children in the control groups, with the signers having a mean IQ of 114 (75th percentile) versus the nonsigners' mean score of 102 (53rd percentile).[1]

Still not convinced? Hopefully, the next chapter will help dispel any reservations you may have.

Chapter 4

Frequently Asked Questions

Q. What if I already know what my baby wants?

A. Babies *are* born with an effective means of communicating their basic needs—*they cry*. When your baby cries, you go through a process of elimination: Is she hungry, wet, tired, or in pain? Usually, after a few tries, you'll hit the right one and she'll stop crying. This, coupled with a good helping of "parent's intuition" actually enables you to meet your baby's basic needs pretty well. So why should you sign?

First of all, signing with your baby saves you a lot of time and lost sleep. Let's say she's crying in the middle of the night. You go to your little angel and nurse and change her. The crying stops while you nurse, but then it starts right up again. After about 45 minutes of this, you get concerned. Is your baby in pain? Is it an ear infection? An intestinal blockage? A burst appendix? Good heavens! Should you take her to the emergency room?

Signing empowers your baby to communicate *specific* things, such as "I have pain in my left ear," "My tummy hurts," or "There's an elephant in my closet!" If your child can indicate to you that she has pain in her left ear, then you could call your pediatrician, who may be able to give you some home-care advice that will ease her discomfort and get you both through until the morning. But imagine rushing your baby to the E.R. in the middle of the night when all you really needed to do was show her that there was no elephant in her closet!

Q. What's the point—won't my baby talk soon anyway?

A. Well, this depends on what you mean by "soon." Soon can seem like a long time when your child is trying to communicate with you by screaming, throwing things, and banging his head against the wall. In general, most babies don't even use "Mama" and "Dada" to the right parent until they're at least 11 months old, and a 12-month-old child who uses two more words *besides* "Mama" and "Dada" is considered in the advanced minority. It takes some time to go from "first words" to "intelligible conversation," and signing not only helps your baby communicate what he can't say, but it also helps him clarify the meaning of what he *is* saying once he starts verbalizing. A child who says "Da" to mean "dog," "Daddy," and "done" can make his meaning clearer by signing while he speaks. Children are encouraged to verbalize *more* when they see that their intended meaning is understood. Eventually, as the child's verbalization of "dog," "Daddy," and "done" become clearer, he'll drop those signs and simply say the words.

Q. Do I have to learn a whole new language?

A. Not at all. As I mentioned before, we call this "baby sign language" because it's the "baby talk"

version of signing. Think about going on a grand European vacation: Would you learn the language of every country you intended to visit? Of course not! But you'd probably try to brush up on a few useful words and phrases for each country you planned to travel to, right? You wouldn't sound very eloquent to the native speakers of those languages, but at least you'd be able to get your basic needs met (except in France, where they'd pretend they couldn't understand you anyway).

When starting to sign with your baby, I suggest choosing between six and ten words to start with and adding more as you feel you and your baby are ready. Parents of young children are *extremely* busy people, and this is exactly why you need early, effective, two-way communication. By empowering your child to communicate her needs, you can ward off frustration and temper tantrums, creating calm and peace in your household, and actually have *more* quality time left to spend with your baby.

Q. How will I find the time to teach my baby?

A. "Teaching" your baby to sign can be compared to teaching your baby to talk. You don't need to put special time aside for signing lessons any more than you would for speaking lessons. As a matter of fact, it's absolutely essential that your baby doesn't suspect that you're trying to "teach" something "special"

or "extra." Signing should be incorporated naturally into your normal day-to-day routines and playtime.

Q. Will signing inhibit my baby's language development?

A. Signing won't inhibit your baby's language development any more than crawling will inhibit his learning to walk. As a matter of fact, research shows that babies who sign generally talk sooner and build vocabulary more quickly than their non-signing peers. In their long-term study, Drs. Linda Acredolo and Susan Goodwyn found that by age 36 months, children who signed as babies were talking at the 47-month age level, putting them nearly a year ahead of their nonsigning peers.[1] Once your baby is physically developed enough to walk, he'll no longer crawl, as walking is a much more efficient means of getting from point A to point B. The same is true of signing and talking—once your baby can say a word clearly enough to make his meaning understood, he'll stop using the sign for that word. Once a child's vocal apparatus are sufficiently developed, plain talking is a lot easier (and you can even do it with your hands full!).

Even when your baby is very young, signing enhances his language development by enhancing word recognition. Imagine looking at your six-month-old and asking him, "Do you want to eat?" Now imagine doing the same thing, but this time you *sign* **EAT** at the same time you *say* "eat." The sign **EAT** is made by miming putting something small into your mouth. Even at nine months of age, children generally recognize only about five to six spoken words, so can you see what a powerful hint your baby is getting when you sign *and* speak at the same time?

Q. How does signing affect early brain development?

A. Everything your baby experiences from the moment she's born, even while sleeping, affects the growth and development within her brain. From the feel of soft pajamas against her skin to the sound of your voice, the life and sensory experiences your baby's exposed to are building the foundation for all future learning.

Your baby is born with billions of brain cells, nearly twice as many as she'll have in adulthood and many more than she'll have even by the age of three. During her first months of life, connecting cells called *synapses* rapidly multiply to the trillions! These cells form pathways between the brain cells and act as transmitters throughout the brain, and these pathways allow learning to occur.[2]

When your baby is exposed to more of a particular type of stimulus—in this case, language stimulus—

more connections are formed in the language center of her brain. When you have a signed interaction with your baby, she receives the message not only auditorially, as with normal speech, but also visually and kinesthetically (that is, physically, through movement or touch), so she's actually receiving the message in triplicate, through three of her senses. When babies receive information in this way consistently, their brains build a more extensive network for dealing with language stimulus, and they tend to learn language better and faster. This can conceivably have a long-term effect on all future language-related learning, including picking up foreign languages and reading and writing skills.

So why do we end up with only half of our brain cells by adulthood? It's largely a case of "use it or lose it": The various life and sensory experiences we're exposed to directly affect which brain cells and synapses live or die. Throughout childhood, Mother Nature chisels away the excess brain cells and synapses to make the brain function more efficiently in adulthood.

The first three years of life—*especially the first year*—are the most crucial for building the foundations of language development, and signing with your baby helps to make the most of this unique window of opportunity!

Q. Aren't American Sign Language (ASL) signs too hard for babies to make?

A. Babies have limited small motor coordination, so in the beginning they won't produce the signs exactly as adults do. Just as your baby hears you say the word *water* but first only manages to say "wa-wa," he'll approximate the gestures he sees you make to the best of his ability. He may, for example, clap or bring his palm to his index finger in an approximation of the sign **MORE,** rather than managing the precise handshape. Just as you understand when your baby says "wa-wa," you'll also learn to recognize his signed approximations.

Now that your questions have been answered, you're probably eager to get started signing with your baby! In the following section, we'll discuss *when to start* signing to your baby, *how to sign* to him, and *how to choose first signs* to use.

So turn the page, and let's get started!

part II

getting started

Chapter 5

When Can You Start?

Six to eight months of age is generally considered an optimal time to start signing with your baby, since before they're six months old, babies have very little long-term memory to retain the signs they see.

Younger babies also lack the motor skills and hand-eye coordination required to make very precise gestures, so parents may miss their babies' early signing attempts, perceiving them as random gestures. Once babies reach six months of age, however, memory retention increases rapidly. If you start signing to them when they're between six and seven months of age, for example, you can reasonably expect them to sign back when they're between eight and ten months old. Older babies and toddlers will generally catch on much more quickly because they're reaching the stage in their development where they begin to imitate, and when they attempt to use gestures to communicate. They may take anywhere from a few days to a few weeks to sign back.

Having said this, there's no harm in starting to sign as early as you like. It's worthwhile to note that deaf parents sign to their babies from birth, and their babies generally sign back significantly earlier than babies in hearing families do. If you're considering starting to sign earlier, just remember that younger babies generally take longer to begin producing signs. In other words, if you start signing to your baby from birth, you might not see his first sign for six long months. This delay may cause you to become discouraged or even give up. If you do decide to start early, the upside is that your baby *could actually be signing back* by six months. One good friend of mine, whose first child took an eternity to sign, started signing with her second child at five months, and he signed back at six months.

So how do you begin? The next chapter will give you the primer you need.

Chapter 6

How to Sign
to Your Baby

Signing to your baby is different from just plain talking to her, so it requires some different strategies. Here we'll discuss ways to get your baby to see your signs, as well as ways to reinforce the meaning of your signs and spoken words.

Get on your baby's level (you should be doing this when you interact with her verbally, too). Get right down on the floor with your child, hold her in your arms or lap, or sit across from her when she's in her high chair. When this isn't possible, angle your sign downward toward her so that she can see it from the intended angle.

Sign in your baby's field of vision. This means signing close to your face, just below your line of sight. Babies are naturally attracted to the human face, so they'll be looking in the direction the speech is coming from.

Say the word. When signing with hearing babies, it's extremely important to always say the word when you sign it. Ultimately, you want your baby to learn to recognize the spoken word without your signing it, and later to learn to say the word herself. You want to make a strong connection between the spoken word and the gesture.

Sign in context. When your baby is first learning a new sign, she needs to experience the sign *in context* to make the association clear to her. For example, don't sign about the **BEAR** you saw *yesterday* at the zoo. Instead, sign about the **BEAR** *while* you're at the zoo: "Hey! Look at the **BEAR!** What a big, fluffy **BEAR!**" Alternately, you could also sign about a **BEAR** in a book or about a teddy **BEAR.**

Sometimes the context is a feeling, such as **PAIN, HOT, COLD, SAD,** or even **MORE.** In these instances your baby needs to be *feeling* the emotion, sensation, or desire for the connection between word and sign to be clearest. Take the sign **MORE,** for example. Let's say your baby is just six months old and is primarily still breast- or bottle-fed. You're starting to give her a little rice cereal once a day, and she isn't all that wild about it. You might be excited to start teaching her the sign **MORE** in the context of **MORE** food, but because your baby isn't feeling a keen yearning for more food, she won't make the connection between your **MORE** sign and a feeling (a yearning for more) that she just doesn't have.

Teach motivating signs. Babies want tools to communicate their needs, desires, interests, feelings, and observations. The signs they'll learn most quickly are ones that are the most motivating to them. In the previous example, the baby is just beginning to eat solid foods. But because this particular baby isn't all that excited about eating yet, **EAT**

or **FOOD** may not be the most motivating signs to teach her at this time. **MILK** would be a better choice, and **MORE** could be taught in the context of **MORE MILK, MORE MUSIC, MORE PLAY,** and so on. (We'll discuss motivating signs more in the next chapter.)

Accompany the sign with the appropriate facial expression. Often the facial expression that accompanies a sign is just as important as the handshape of the sign. For example, the sign for **SCARED** or **FEAR** is accompanied by a startled expression. When parents practice this sign in my classes, they often have either a bland or amused expression on their faces. When I stand in front of the class and mirror back to them what this looks like, it usually brings down the house. Try going to a mirror and practicing the **SCARED** sign with different faces, and you'll see what I mean. (The other members of your household will wonder what all that hysterical laughing coming from the bathroom is about!) When you sign to your baby, exaggerating your facial expression makes your meaning much clearer. If your baby laughs at you, all the better—you're making learning fun!

There isn't always an obvious facial expression for a sign; sometimes there's no specific expression required, while other times the expression varies according to the context. For example, what facial expression goes with **MILK?** Well, if you're nursing your baby, you might hold your hand close to your face and sign **MILK** while saying, "Mmm, that's good **MILK!**" You'd probably just instinctively smile at your baby while saying this, since that would be the natural expression for commenting on something being good. If you were offering her **MILK**—as in, "Do you want **MILK?**"—you'd want to be sure to really exaggerate the raised eyebrows of your "questioning face" and tone of your voice. When you do this, your baby is not only learning the sign for **MILK,** but she's also learning another valuable language skill: what a question looks and sounds like. [ASL note: Questions such as "what" and "where" are accompanied by lowered eyebrows, while "yes or no" questions are accompanied by raised eyebrows.]

Include signing naturally during daily routines and playtime. I can't stress enough how important it is to keep your signing fun and easygoing. If your baby senses that you're stressed out and desperate for his attention, he'll tend to shut you out. It's far better to allow your baby to "absorb" signs naturally, without realizing he's being taught anything.

Let's say, for example, that you're giving your baby a bath. **WATER, WASH,** and **DUCK** might be words that pop up frequently at bath time. Here's how *not* to sign with your baby:

"Look sweetheart, this is *WATER*, okay? When you want *WATER*, do this for Mommy. Sweetie, look at Mommy; look here, over here, sweetie! *WATER!*" (Mom anxiously pleads with her son to look at her signing. Baby tunes her out—Mommy's game is not fun.)

Now here's a better idea:

"Oh, my goodness! Look at all this **WATER**! Should we splash the **WATER**? Look, here comes your **DUCKY**! What does your **DUCKY** say? Quack! Quack! Can you **WASH** your **DUCKY**?" (Mom is smiling and relaxed, and so is Baby.)

In the latter example, mother and child are inter-acting happily and naturally with each other. The mother engages her child enthusiastically in what she's talking and signing about, integrating learning into playing.

By now, you're probably ready to try signing—but which signs should you use first? The next chap-ter will help you tackle that question.

Chapter 7

Choosing
First Signs

When choosing first signs, I like to use the system developed by Drs. Michelle Anthony and Reyna Lindert, of **www.wideeyedlearning.com,**[1] for use with the families they teach in their signing play-class program. In the *Signing Smart™ Beginner Handbook* that accompanies the beginner class, Anthony and Lindert suggest starting by choosing three to five signs from each of the following two categories:

1. See a Lot/Do a Lot Signs. These are signs for things that happen repeatedly throughout the day; that is, things you *see and do a lot*. Signs having to do with daily routines are good choices, such as **DIAPER, CHANGE, EAT, DRINK,** and so forth. See a Lot/Do a Lot

Signs are often the ones that we parents are the most excited (read: *desperate*) for our children to learn, because they're the ones that have the potential to help us more easily meet our children's basic needs and ward off a lot of crying and whining in the process. Repeating the same signs over and over is good practice for you and your baby and helps you get into the habit of signing. Babies learn best through repetition, and repeating signs helps them make a strong connection between sign, occurrence, and spoken word.

2. Highly Motivating Signs: These are the signs for things that are important to your child and fun for him; that is, things that your baby really loves or gets excited about. Signs for toys, family pets or other animals, cars, babies, music, and so forth make great Highly Motivating Signs. These signs are the most important ones from your baby's point of view, because, as Anthony and Lindert point out, "Highly Motivating Signs enable children to comment on things and initiate conversations about things that interest them and that they have no other way to communicate."[1]

If your baby is hungry or wet, all he has to do is cry—you'll run through the short list of possible causes and figure out which one it is fairly quickly. Now let's say, for example, that you take your baby for a walk around the neighborhood, and at one point you visit with a neighbor's cat. The cat is very friendly, and your baby really enjoys seeing and touching it. Later (perhaps even a couple of days later), your baby decides that he'd like to see the cat again or maybe just hear more about cats in general. How can he bring up this topic of conversation? He can cry all he likes, but Mommy probably won't guess "wants cat" as a possible cause of his distress. Using Highly Motivating Signs will teach your baby the power of signing and get him interested in *all* the signs you're showing him.

Clever parents can make See a Lot/Do a Lot Signs into Highly Motivating Signs by integrating them into playtime. If baby just loves his teddy bear, take it and say, "Teddy is hungry. Should we give him some **FOOD (EAT)?**" or "Teddy needs a diaper **CHANGE!**"

By using signing with playtime, you can make virtually any sign a Highly Motivating Sign and turn quality time with your child into *super* quality time!

Finally, the day arrives when your child produces his first sign. Once he does, you're over the first hurdle—all of your perseverance has paid off, and you're seeing some concrete proof that your baby is really getting it!

Over the next few weeks, your baby will gradually add more signs. Once he has somewhere between five to ten signs, he'll have reached what Anthony and Lindert describe as "the sign cluster," which will appear as a "signing epiphany" of sorts. Suddenly, your baby will begin signing more often and more spontaneously, and he'll sometimes pop up with signs you haven't shown him in weeks. He'll also begin to learn new signs easily, and may even begin to point at things and ask for the sign with a **WHAT?** gesture. (My own daughter did this even though I hadn't intentionally taught her the sign for **WHAT?** I must make that gesture involuntarily a lot!) At this point, the only limit on how many signs your baby can learn is how many you can show him. Just know that parents often find themselves scrambling to keep up with their children's demand for more signs.

Signing with your baby requires more than just learning and using signs—it also requires some creative strategizing on your part. Parents often find it difficult initially to get their baby to "pay attention" and see their signs. Even hearing parents who come from a signing background, such as professional ASL interpreters, are often at a loss as to how to successfully convey signs to their infants. In the following section, we'll discuss how to use signing strategies specific to babies and toddlers.

part III

now you're
signing!

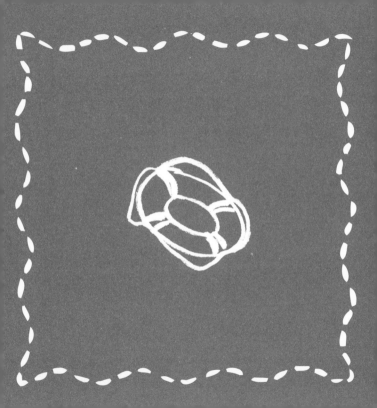

Chapter 8

Lifesaver
Signs

The following are what I like to call the "Ten Lifesaver Signs," which can be used to ward off a world of trouble. (I've also included some creative signing strategies that can be employed to teach some of these signs *before* disaster strikes.)

1. **COLD.** A great way to teach this sign is by using a chilled teething ring. Give it to your baby and sign **COLD** repeatedly as she mouths it. In *Sign with your Baby*, author Joseph Garcia recommends using bowls of warm and cold water to teach temperature signs.

2. **GENTLE.** When baby is pulling the family pet's fur or ears, sign **GENTLE** by stroking her arm and your own in turn.

3. **HELP.** When you notice that your baby is having a hard time with something, ask, "Do you want **HELP?**" and then help her.

4. **HOT.** You can use the **HOT** sign with things that are only a little bit hot, such as a warm sidewalk or playground equipment in summer. You can also use it as a warning, paired with **PAIN** and **NO TOUCH** when referring to the stove, barbeque, and so forth. You might even pretend to burn yourself while cooking and sign **HOT** and **PAIN.**

With any luck, you'll never get the opportunity to teach **HOT** in the true context of "burning hot," but if your baby does receive a minor burn, try to remember to sign **HOT** and **PAIN** while you administer first aid and kisses. (Seemingly minor burns can be very serious for babies and toddlers and often require skin grafts if not treated immediately. If your child burns herself and you have any doubt at all, call the burn unit at your local hospital immediately.)

5. **NO.** Here's a handy sign! Many parents continue to find this sign useful throughout their children's growing years. It's a lot nicer to flash your child a warning **NO** sign than to shout across

the room at her, especially in mixed company or places where you need to be quiet, such as in church.

6. **NO TOUCH.** It can be useful to pair **NO** and **TOUCH,** although babies usually know why you're signing just plain **NO** when they're headed for Grandma's glass reindeer collection.

7. **PAIN.** Be sure to use this sign whenever you, your baby, or anyone is hurting or is wearing a bandage. Always sign **PAIN** at the actual site of the pain so that your baby will learn to localize the sign and will be able to show you where it hurts. Sign **PAIN** as an integral part of kissing your child's

"boo-boos" better, as a warning about things that can hurt, and to express empathy for someone else who's in pain. (Pretending to bump your head and stub your toe also works here.) For families who aren't accident-prone, teething time provides a great opportunity to use the **PAIN** sign.

8. **SCARED** or **FEAR.** If something startles or scares your baby, be sure to use this sign while talking about her fear. Sirena really enjoyed being startled—she'd jump a mile and then laugh with glee when my husband or I would jump out from a corner and say "Boo!" Of course you don't want to do this unless your baby loves it. You can just wait until something like the Cookie Monster on

Sesame Street or an alligator at the zoo scares your baby, and then show her the **SCARED (SCARY, FEAR, AFRAID)** sign.

9. **SHARE.** You can use this sign whenever you find yourself mediating between two children who are tussling over a toy, or when you share food with your baby. Break off a piece of your banana and sign **SHARE** before handing your baby a piece. This sign can also be flashed as a warning when you see trouble a-brewin' in the playground.

10. **STOP.** This is a great safety sign. There are a lot of games you can play with the signs **STOP** and **GO** (see Chapter 19). Try to play **STOP** and **GO**

games often to teach your baby what these signs mean early on. **STOP** also provides some variety for parents who are tired of saying and signing **NO** all the time.

Chapter 9

Attention-Getting Strategies

Parents who are skeptical about trying signing are often concerned that their babies won't pay attention to them, since their babies' eyes are all over the place and they won't sit still.

If this sounds like your baby, and it probably does, I have some good news: Babies don't need to "pay attention"—at least not as we know it. I once actually saw my daughter learn a sign through her ear. I'm not kidding. (Well, maybe there was some *very* peripheral vision involved, but it didn't seem like it!) Here's what happened.

Sirena and I were enjoying a walk in the park (she was in her stroller) with my friend Cheryl and her baby when a squirrel ran onto the path. This was my baby's first squirrel, so I quickly signed **SQUIRREL** to her, trying to take advantage of this *in-context teaching opportunity*. I signed again and again, but do you think she would look at me? No way! She was craning her head all over the place trying to see around the bush the squirrel had run into.

Cheryl gave me bit of a ribbing. "Oh yeah, sure—she's *really* paying attention to you!"

I gave up, and we continued on our walk. About 20 minutes later, another squirrel ran out of the bushes. Sirena turned around in her stroller, looked right at me, and signed **SQUIRREL.**

Cheryl and I were dumbfounded. "She didn't even look at you before!" Cheryl exclaimed.

"I know!" I said. "What did she do, see me sign through her ear?"

The point of the story is this: Don't stress about whether or not your baby is looking at your signs. Signing often—*whether your baby is looking at you or not*—will give you the practice you need to feel comfortable, and you'll also make signing a habit. At the same time, you'll be surprised by how much of your signing your baby actually *does* see, even when she doesn't appear to be paying attention.

There are some great strategies you can use to increase the chance of your child seeing your signs, many of which have been learned by watching deaf mothers interact with their babies. Just as hearing parents raise the pitch of their voices to get their child's attention, deaf parents modify their signing and use various other attention-getting tactics while interacting with their babies.

The following are some great ways to help your baby see your signs:

Verbally get their attention. Call your child's name or use a term of endearment: "Hey, Punkin, look at Mommy!"

Seize the moment. Sometimes you and your baby will just look at each other spontaneously, for no particular reason, which is what *Sign with your Baby* author Joseph Garcia terms the "Chance Mutual Gaze." When this happens, you could just grab a nearby toy or other object that might interest your baby, and model the sign for it—for example, "Do you want your **BALL** (or **BOOK** or **BEAR**)?"

Lie in wait. Sometimes the best way to get your baby to look at you is to do nothing at all. If you sit there watching your baby play, he'll look up at you from time to time as if to say, "Are you *still* watching me?" This is what Garcia terms the "Expressive Gaze," when your baby wants to express a feeling or ask a question.[1] This is the perfect time to sign about whatever it is he's playing with. Example: "You have your **BEAR.** Are you **HUGGING** your **BEAR?**"

Share experiences spontaneously. Oftentimes, you and your baby will look at the same thing and then at each other. This is what Garcia terms the "Pointed Gaze," and once you know about it you'll notice it happening a lot. Imagine if you went out for a walk with your baby and a crow squawked loudly from the overhead wire. You'd both probably look up at the bird and then at each other, as if to say, "Did you hear that?" This would be a perfect time to say and sign **HEAR** and then point at the bird and say and sign **BIRD.**

Get physical. Videotapes of deaf mothers interacting with their children show the mothers actively seeking their babies' attention by gently but persistently tapping their hands or other parts of their bodies.[2] Tapping your child's hands when you want him to sign back reminds him that there's something you expect him to do with his hands. You can also stroke or rub him to get his attention—stroking his cheek with a finger, for example, will often get him to turn toward you.

Let your baby see the object and your sign at the same time. At first, you'll find that this is easier said than done. Previously, I instructed you to sign close to your face, in your baby's field of vision. With babies, these two things do not always go together. Children don't appreciate having their play interrupted and their attention commandeered to learn signs. Smart parents learn to adapt their signing so that their children can see the sign and the corresponding object while continuing their play.

✗ ✗ ✗

Here are some strategies to use while playing and interacting with your child:

Sign on your child's body. With some signs, it's just as effective for your baby to feel the sensation of the sign on his body as it is to actually see the sign. The sign for **PET** or **GENTLE** is a great example: If your child is playing with a cat, you could tell him to **PET** the cat or be **GENTLE** by stroking his arm instead of your own. (Stroking the forearm is the sign for both **PET** and **GENTLE**.) Clearly your child doesn't need to look at his arm to know what's happening, and his attention is allowed to remain on the cat. Some other signs that work well are **BEAR, COW, DOG,** or **TELEPHONE.**

Put your sign between your child and the object or toy he's interested in. You can either come in from the side or reach around your child with both hands. This works well with signs that only require the use of your hands, such as **BALL, SHOES,** or **MORE.**

Pass objects between yourself and your child. Pick up an object that interests him, bring it toward yourself, produce the sign for it, and then pass it to your child. His eyes will usually track the object long enough for you to produce the sign and pass it back to him. You can pass the object between you like this more than once, signing the name of the object, **PLEASE** and **THANK YOU,** and so on.

Chapter 10

Positive
Reinforcement

Babies' early attempts at signing are often vague and easy to miss. Parents frequently tell me that they *think* their child may be signing, but they're not sure. If your baby is clapping every time she finishes her food, she's very likely signing her version of the **MORE** sign (I'll talk more about *approximations* like this in the next chapter).

When your baby makes any motion that resembles a sign, even if you think it was accidental, be sure to respond to it as if it was indeed a deliberate sign. It's very important to positively reinforce her efforts—if it wasn't a sign, then nothing's lost; if it *was* an actual attempt to sign, then you've just communicated a very important message: that what she's doing is right and that you're paying attention to her efforts to communicate.

When your baby is first learning a sign, you should try to reward her efforts whenever possible. If your baby signs **EAT,** try giving her a cracker or a few Cheerios, even if it isn't snacktime. If she signs **MILK,** give her a small bottle or nurse her for a few minutes. Children who receive positive reinforcement for their early signing efforts will realize the power of signing more quickly and will attempt to sign more often.

But what happens when your baby's signs don't come out perfectly? That's the topic of our next chapter.

Chapter 11

Signing
Mistakes

Young babies and toddlers don't have the motor skills required to make very precise handshapes yet. It's also very difficult for them to coordinate two movements at once. Think about all those "baby-safe" lids and latches you have installed in your home—even adults have a hard time with some of these! So because of these two factors, your baby will *approximate* many of the signs she sees you make.

Some commonly used handshapes for babies are:

- An extended index finger

- An open hand with all five fingers extended

- Four fingers extended

- A closed fist

For example, your baby may clap, bang her fists together, or put her index finger to her palm to sign **MORE** rather than producing the precise "flat 0" hand-shape. When using signs with difficult "Y" handshapes, such as **I LOVE YOU, PLAY,** or **AIRPLANE** your child may simply use her open hand(s), as if waving.

Your baby may also have trouble coordinating the movement of a sign with its handshape and will often make much bigger movements or leave the movement out entirely. For example, for **FINISHED** or **ALL DONE,** your baby may wave her entire arms back and forth instead of the smaller flipping-over-the-hands motion. When signing **CAT,** she may just pinch her cheeks, omitting the outward "whisker tracing" movement of the sign.

Because many of your baby's early signing attempts will use these few easier-to-make handshapes, many of her signs will look the same at first. This can be frustrating, but here are some ways you can narrow down her meanings:

- **Location:** Your child may use her open hand to sign **COW** on the side of her head, **AIRPLANE** above her head, **MOMMY** on front of her face, and **I LOVE YOU** to one side of her face. Although the handshape is the same, the location changes the meaning.

- **Movement:** Your baby may use the same handshape but vary the movement, providing an additional clue as to her meaning. She may wave both open hands in front of her torso for **PLAY,** bounce the same open hands for **BALL,** and wave her open hands back and forth for **FINISHED** or **ALL DONE.**

- **Gaze:** Where is your child looking? She may be looking at what she wants **MORE** of or at the object she's signing about.

- **Context:** Look around and assess the situation, then take a guess. The important thing is that you respond positively to your child's efforts. Even if you don't always get it exactly right, she'll know that you're paying attention, and that you're happy and proud she's trying to communicate with you.

When your baby approximates or makes up her own version of a sign, be sure to continue to model the correct sign yourself, as this will give her the repeated opportunity to see the correct version she's striving for. Eventually her dexterity will improve and her signs will most likely become more like yours. If this doesn't happen, don't worry. *You* know what your baby is telling you, and that's what's really important here.

Using the Wrong Sign

Sometimes children will overgeneralize with signs. For example, your baby may want **MILK,** and she knows that by opening and closing her fists, she'll get what she wants, so she'll try the **MILK** sign to get *whatever* she wants. In other words, **MILK** means **I WANT.** (Some children may also use **MORE** to mean **I WANT.**)

When your child overgeneralizes like this, you can take advantage of the opportunity by modeling both the sign she's misusing and a more appropriate sign in the correct context. For example, if your child is signing **MORE,** but she really wants **FOOD,** you can say, "Do you want something to **EAT?**" and give her a few Cheerios. Wait until she's finished eating, then ask, "Do you want **MORE** Cheerios?"

Sometimes you may think your child is using the wrong sign, but keep in mind that children see so many things that we adults just don't notice. Once Sirena and I were at an indoor swimming pool and she kept signing **BIRD** to me. I scanned the walls for pictures of birds. Finding none, I told my daughter, "There are no birdies. Birdies are outside."

Sirena was still insistent, nodding her head and signing **BIRD** again. Finally I asked, "Where is the **BIRD?**" She pointed to a gym bag on a bench quite far away. By squinting, I was able make out a tiny label with a picture of a parrot on it. I'd found Sirena's **BIRD.**

Sirena also found three **KITTIES (CAT)** holding up the curtain above Mommy and Daddy's bed. Actually, they're supposed to be clusters of ivy, but now when I lie in bed looking up, I can't see them as anything other than the **KITTIES** Sirena sees.

Another time, my daughter used **MOON** to describe a crescent-shaped, dried eucalyptus leaf hanging from a spiderweb on a swing set. Clearly she knew that the leaf wasn't a moon, but it did look like one: a tiny, shimmering golden moon, slowly turning on the breeze—a moon grown-ups couldn't see without the help of a child's eyes.

And just know that sometimes your baby's broad use of signs can make you scream with laughter. One summer our family was staying at a bed-and-breakfast while attending my sister's wedding in Northern California. On the ground floor, there was a very romantic patio restaurant, which Sirena and her daddy were walking through early one evening. As they passed near a table occupied by a voluptuous

109

woman in a *very* low-cut blouse, my daughter, who was walking in front of my husband, gave the woman the once-over and then proceeded to sign **MILK** repeatedly as they passed her table. Of course my husband almost fell on the floor right there. Once they got back to the room, it took him ten minutes before he could stop laughing long enough to tell me what had happened!

Chapter 12

Made-Up
Signs

While I recommend sticking with ASL signs most of the time, there are some instances when it's practical to make up a sign. Made-up signs are commonly referred to as "home signs" and are even used in deaf families—although they're generally discontinued by the time the children start school.

Maybe you have a Grandma *and* a Nana whom you spend a lot of time with, so you need a different sign for each. You could use **GRANDMA** for one, and make up a sign for Nana. Or perhaps you have two dogs or three cats and you'd like to make up different signs to tell them apart. Other times you'll have an in-context teaching opportunity that you just won't want to miss. Even if you carry a small ASL dictionary around with you, which I strongly recommend, no dictionary has a sign for *everything* in it. For instance, my family lives very close to the world-famous San Diego Zoo and Sea World Adventure Park—I take my daughter to both places a lot, and we tend to make up animal signs for the more exotic species.

Having said all this, I want to caution you against making up too many signs—and when you do, you should record an accurate representation of them that can be understood not only by you, but also by others who care for your child. If you don't do this, you're going to forget the signs you made up . . . but your baby won't. When this happens, you'll really feel stupid, believe me. Sirena would be trying to sign something to me about a recent zoo trip, and for the life of me I wouldn't be able to remember which animal it was. She'd look at me as if to say, "Are you making this up as you go along or what?" *Oops!* Caught red-handed by my one-year-old!

Babies will also make up their own signs from time to time, which is something that comes naturally to all babies, whether they sign or not. For instance, my daughter made up her own signs for **BLANKET** and **OPEN** (as in, "Open a container"). Her made-up signs were so incredibly expressive that we opted to use them instead of the actual ASL versions of **BLANKET** and **OPEN.**

When your baby makes up a sign, you can either opt to keep it and put it into normal use, or you can respond by saying the word and signing the correct

ASL version. As with sign approximations, your child's version of the sign will tend to become more like yours as he sees you use your version repeatedly. When deciding whether or not to use a made-up sign, consider what, if any, effect using a made-up sign for that particular item will have in your child's life.

For example, a child who attends a preschool or child-care program where signing is used probably won't run into many problems using a made-up sign for **SEA OTTER,** as sea otters just don't occur all that often in preschool. However, using made-up signs for **POTTY, HELP, EAT,** or even **COW** could cause some confusion and frustration at school. Even having a special "pet sign" for that **BLANKET** or **PACIFIER** can cause big problems. It's generally best to stick with actual

ASL signs for routine objects and actions, as well as things that are very important to your baby. And deaf or hard-of-hearing children (or children who have deaf or hard-of-hearing family members or close friends) should stick strictly to ASL to limit confusion.

From time to time, parents ask me if it's too late to change a sign to ASL if they've already taught their child a made-up version. I had to do quite a bit of this with my own daughter, and in my experience, changing signs later in the game doesn't cause any long-term bewilderment, as babies and toddlers are incredibly adaptable. Just tell and show your baby that you have a new sign for that object or action, and start using the new sign in place of the old one. He'll quickly get the hang of it, just as he does when he makes up a sign and you teach him the correct version, or when the whole family uses a "baby talk" word with him and then later switches to the adult version. Of course it's easiest to teach the correct ASL version in the first place whenever possible.

Since my daughter has begun talking, my husband and I have taught her the proper ASL versions of most of the signs we made up. Sirena communicates by talking now, but I'm constantly amazed at how well she remembers the signs she's learned and by her continued interest in learning new signs. I'd like her to go on to learn ASL as a second language, so I want her to know the correct signs. She already has such a great head start!

chapter 13

Setting
Limits

Eventually your baby will be happily and enthusiastically using signs to get most of her needs met: When she wants to nurse, she'll smile at you and sign **MILK;** when she wants something opened for her, she'll sign **HELP** before frustration sets in. Most of the time these exchanges will be free of tears, but what happens when it's time to cut out that 2-A.M. feeding? While you do want to reinforce early signing by responding to your baby's requests, there will come a time when your baby has to learn a harsh truth: *Just because she can sign what she wants doesn't always mean she'll get what she wants.*

Cutting out Sirena's 2-A.M. feedings nearly broke my heart. I'd go into her room, and she'd be standing in her crib desperately signing **MILK**. Eventually this escalated into crying *and* signing, and I did briefly consider that maybe it would have been easier if I could pretend I didn't know what she wanted. Thankfully, this phase was short-lived, and the benefits far outweighed the heartache.

Once your baby knows a sign for something, it's perfectly reasonable *and necessary* for parents to set limits. If your baby signs **EAT,** for example, you could reply by saying and signing, "I see you're signing **EAT**. We will **EAT** soon. Right now let's look at your **BOOK**." By responding in this way, you acknowledge your child's request without giving into it. You're also mirroring back her signs and offering (and signing) an alternative.

Children are going to test for limits, and they'll continue to do so until you show them where the limits are. Signing babies really do want to know if signing will always get them what they want, so using signs such as **SHARE, STOP, GENTLY, NO,** and **SIT** will help teach them limits and give them a way to express limits themselves. For example, a child who can sign **STOP** or **SHARE** while interacting with other children will be much less likely to resort to hitting or biting. Preschool and child-care programs that use signing find that it dramatically reduces aggressive behavior in the classroom.

While signing with babies does cut down dramatically on the frustration, crying, and tantrums that result from not being able to communicate, it won't completely eliminate the "terrible twos." Your signing toddler will still be likely to throw a screaming tantrum when she doesn't get her way. Nobody's found a cure for that one yet!

Chapter 14

Combining
Signs

As your baby's signing vocabulary expands, he'll eventually begin combining two or more signs into mini-sentences. This represents a major milestone in your baby's language development and expands his ability to communicate increasingly complex ideas and concepts.

For example, your baby will often combine the sign **MORE** with whatever it is he'd like **MORE** of: **MORE + COOKIE** or **MORE + MILK.** However, sign combinations such as **HOT + NO + TOUCH** or **BALL + PLAY + DADDY** really take signing to the next level. At this stage, your child is recognizing words and is able to use them in the correct context—all that remains is for his vocal apparatus to catch up, and he'll be off and talking!

As your child begins to talk, he'll also begin to combine *spoken* words with signs. He may combine a word he *can* say with the sign for a word he *can't* yet say, such as, "Birdie" + **UP** or **WHERE** + "Daddy." As your child begins to do this, you may find that he communicates so effectively that you won't remember which words he actually says and which ones he signs!

Your baby will also continue to use signs as needed for clarification or emphasis in the early stages of talking. When he first begins to speak, for example, his spoken versions of "dog" and "doll" may sound a lot alike. Using signs to clarify the meaning of words often helps alleviate a lot of frustration, and encourages him to verbalize even more.

Chapter 15

Stumbling Blocks

As you go along, you may find that some obstacles keep cropping up in your path. This chapter focuses on how to deal with common stumbling blocks in baby sign language.

Starting with Too Few Signs

Parents who start with too few signs may do so out of concern that their child will get confused or "overloaded" by being exposed to too many signs at once. Fear not: *As long as you're consistent* in signing the words you've chosen, your baby won't become overwhelmed from seeing a lot of signing. As a matter of fact, children who see a lot of signing generally get the hang of it much more quickly.

Once again, you can compare learning to sign with learning to speak. After all, do you say to your spouse, "Okay, honey, let's just use these three words around the baby, and when she can say those, we'll add more—we don't want to overload her with too much talking"? Of course not! You talk and read to your baby as much as possible, and the more you do, the better and faster her language development comes along. Deaf parents sign every word, all the time—and do their children become confused? No. These children actually begin producing signs much earlier than children from hearing families because they learn to sign by total immersion.

When you start with too few signs, you won't sign enough to become comfortable with signing and make it a habit. Your baby won't get used to looking to you for signing, and he won't have the opportunity to learn signs by seeing you modeling them repeatedly. As we discussed in Chapter 7, choosing three to five signs for things that you frequently see and do each day will ensure that you have signs that can be repeated often during the course of your baby's daily routines.

Starting with Too Many Signs to Be Consistent

Once you realize how fun and easy it is to sign, you may be tempted to start using every sign in this book all at once—however, it's much more effective to use a few signs consistently than it is to use every sign you can think of whenever you remember to do it.

What might your baby be thinking if you only occasionally produce the **MILK** sign when you offer it? "What's Mommy doing with her hand?" she might wonder. "Is it something to do with milk? No, that can't be it—she didn't do that the last time I nursed."

Your baby will make the connection more easily when you sign consistently.

Overanticipating Baby's Needs

Because you can often tell what your baby wants, even without signing, you may tend to over-anticipate her needs. You can see that the pile of Cheerios on her high chair's tray has run out and she's starting to whine a little—clearly she wants **MORE.** Because you want to prevent the situation from escalating into crying, you're likely to rush in immediately with more Cheerios. But if you've been working on the **MORE** sign with your baby, you can first try to give her some hints and encouragement as to how she can more effectively get her needs met.

For example, ask your baby, "**WHAT** do you want?

Can you show me with your hands?" (Tap her hands.) "Do you want **MORE?**" (Sign **MORE.**) Then give her more Cheerios, whether or not she's responded to your efforts. You can also try to mold her hand into the shape of the sign if she'll let you—but you should stop if this seems to annoy her at all, as you want to keep this fun and lighthearted.

Not Using Motivating Signs

I can't stress enough how important it is to use signs that are motivating to your baby. If she doesn't feel a strong need or desire to communicate something, she'll be much less likely to use the sign for it.

The signs your baby will sign back most quickly are the ones she's absolutely *desperate* to communicate. (For more on this, please refer back to Chapter 7.)

chapter 16

Including Caregivers, Family, and Friends

Anyone who cares for or regularly interacts with your child can and should be involved in signing with him. The more you can get family members, friends, and caregivers in on it, the better your baby's signing will come along.

Signing with Family Members

Sometimes parents run into resistance from other family members. A misinformed but well-meaning grandparent may be concerned that a signing child who can just use his hands may become "too lazy" to talk, for instance; or a spouse may mistakenly believe that signing may stigmatize the child as "slow" or disabled. Some dads may not take the idea of baby sign language seriously or consider it something that's in "Mom's department."

It can often be difficult to get these people to read a book when they already have a negative or passive mind-set, so a really great way to win them over is to bring them to a baby sign language class or show them an instructional video that includes babies actually signing. *Sign with your Baby* is a great video for this purpose, and it can be purchased separately or as part of a complete learning kit.[1] (You can find these materials listed in the Resources section of this book, or by going to **www.sign2me.com.**)

Even skeptical family members will most likely be won over once they see your baby actually start to sign—they won't be able to resist having that kind of close, communicative relationship with him, too.

Signing and Child Care

Many working parents would love to sign with their babies, but they're concerned about how signing will fit into the child-care picture. If your child will be spending most of his day in someone else's care, then the other caregiver(s) should most definitely be involved in his signing program as well.

Many child-care and preschool programs are starting to include signing as an integral part of their curriculum. Early childhood educators who keep up on current research in the field of child development know that signing with the children in their care not only makes life easier and happier for the children, but it's also easier and happier for the staff. In fact, I'm regularly asked to speak to large groups of early-childhood professionals and educators, and I frequently teach private classes for parents and staff at child-care and preschool programs.

When searching for a child-care or preschool program for your child, start looking early, and ask each program director if any signing is used with the children in their program. If the answer is no, ask if they'd be willing to learn and use certain signs with your child. If they've never heard of signing with hearing children, you could explain the benefits, lend them this book, tell them about any classes in your area, or even ask if they'd be willing to watch a video (if you have one).

Occasionally, you're going to run across a child-care provider or program director who's resistant to or even hostile when it comes to the idea of signing with babies, usually because they're either misinformed or uneducated about the topic. If you run into a situation where the person in charge isn't receptive to the idea of signing with babies, cross them off your list of possible child-care providers. In my view, these people don't have the best interests of children at heart. The benefits of signing with babies are clearly proven, but sometimes you can't teach an old dog new tricks. Some administrators just get so mired in the paperwork end of things that they don't keep up with the latest research and developments in early childhood education . . . nor do they have any interest in doing so.

Nannies are a great option if you can afford one. Younger nannies and au pairs are often enthusiastic, receptive to new ideas, and eager to expand their credentials with more education; and older, more experienced nannies have done enough hands-on child rearing to really understand the benefits of signing. As a matter of fact, when I have an information table or booth at a baby store or family event, the people who approach my table most often are older parents, adoptive or foster parents (who are often more mature), and grandparents. These people have been around children long enough to really understand the potential benefits that signing offers.

When you interview a nanny or babysitter, arrange some time to explain your child's signing program in detail, showing some video or getting your baby to demonstrate if possible. Mark the signs your child uses right in this book so that the caregiver can reference them easily. You might even consider copying and posting a few of the pictures from this book in relevant areas, for example, mealtime signs near the high chair. *Sign with your Baby* has special laminated posters just for this purpose, in various signing themes.[2]

Signing with Friends and Peers

Parents often ask me if young babies will actually sign to each other. Sirena and I have been members of the same play group since she was only a few weeks old. Most of the babies were born within a few months of each other, and like me, many of the mothers signed with their babies.

Initially, we'd looked forward to sitting around the playground, watching our babies carry on conversations with their little hands. As we've since learned, babies aren't all that interested in interacting with each other. When they play, they engage in *parallel play,* which means that they'll play *next* to each other rather than actively *with* each other. Little babies are actually far more interested in interacting with adults. Maybe this is nature's way of avoiding "the blind leading the blind," so to speak. Whatever the reason, don't expect a lot of signing between younger babies.

On occasion, however, the other mothers and I *have* witnessed a few signed interactions between our babies. When Sirena was still too young to walk, for instance, another mother and I saw my daughter signing **MILK** to this woman's son. Both of us moms were still nursing, so we found this really amusing. What was Sirena doing—recommending my milk to another baby? "Hey, you should try my mom's milk. It's the best!"

As the children in our group have moved from babyhood to toddlerhood, we've witnessed them signing to each other more. Some of them have learned to sign **SHARE,** for example, instead of just grabbing toys from other children. They've sometimes signed interactions about the toys they're playing with or the experiences they're sharing. In addition, many of the mothers have prompted their children to use **PLEASE, SORRY,** and **THANK YOU** with the other children (and adults) when appropriate.

When Sirena first started using signs with other children, I worried that her feelings would be hurt if she signed to a child who didn't know how to sign back. I felt bad for her when she walked up to another child and signed **PLAY,** only to get a blank stare in return. Now that she's a talker, however, I realize that this is just how toddlers and preschoolers often are—

they don't have all the social graces in place yet. Sirena now walks up to a child she doesn't know and *says,* "My name is Sirena. Do you want to play?" (More often than not, she still gets the same blank stare in response.)

This leads to the inevitable question: What happens to signing after your child starts to speak? That's what the next chapter is all about.

Chapter 17

Is There Signing
After Talking?

"Will my baby continue to sign after she can talk?" is a common question parents ask in my classes. In general, babies will use the tools they have for as long as they need them. As children begin to speak, there's a short period of "overlap" when they simultaneously say *and* sign certain words.

A baby who knows how to sign **MORE,** for example, will use that sign for preverbal communication and will likely continue to use it as she begins to attempt to verbalize the word *more.* She'll continue to use the sign to clarify the meaning of the spoken word until she knows you can understand her easily. Eventually your baby will drop the sign for **MORE,** but she may still use it for emphasis on occasion.

For example, sometimes I'd be washing dishes or be otherwise occupied, and my daughter would announce, "I want **MORE** juice, Mommy!" If I didn't whip my gloves off right away and get her the juice (which there's no way I'd do), Sirena would put her hands in front of my face and repeatedly say *and* sign **MORE,** as if to say, "Maybe you can't hear me, so let me spell it out for you: I want **MORE!**"

Some parents have high hopes that their children will continue to sign as a second language, but children will do what their parents, and later their peers, do. If you continue to sign *and* talk, then your baby might do the same for a time. Most hearing parents, however, tend to drop the signs as soon as their babies learn them, and their babies drop the signs as they begin to talk.

Toddlers can be taught to continue to use signs with deaf or hard-of-hearing family members if they spend enough time with them. Just as babies in bilingual households can learn that they must always use Spanish with Grandpa, signing children will use the tools they have to communicate when they need to.

Sometimes parents who have begun signing with their older toddlers want to introduce signs for words that their children can already say. In my experience, toddlers who can talk won't use signs for words that they can already say well. Because it's easier to simply say the word, they have no motivation to sign it. (Children of all ages, however, enjoy using signs along with songs, even with words they can say.)

Many hearing families continue to find signing useful long after their children can speak, and there are many situations where signing may actually be preferred to talking. For example, a parent can flash **I LOVE YOU** across the track, playing field, or pool when their child performs well in a sporting event (the vast majority of older children and teens prefer this approach to Mom standing in the bleachers screaming, "Mommy loves you, sweetie!"); or a parent or child can sign **POTTY** or **TOILET** in mixed company without risking embarrassment.

Sirena is three years old now, and she talks a mile a minute and can say just about anything. Still, I'm constantly amazed by how many signs she still remembers. Occasionally I catch her signing with her dolls or stuffed animals, and she stills enjoys signing along with songs and playing signing games. As I mentioned before, I'd love to enroll her in an ASL class as soon as she's old enough, for she's already had a great head start in a valuable skill.

chapter 18

The
Greatest Gift

When all is said (or *signed*) and done, the greatest benefit of signing with your baby isn't increased IQ, enhanced language development, or the ability to meet his needs more quickly and with less crying. In my opinion, the greatest benefits of signing are emotional: allowing open communication and mutual understanding, and deepening the bonds of love and trust between parent and child like nothing else.

Children who learn to sign early on find out that they're loved, that they're valued members of the family, and that their thoughts and ideas are important. Is there any better message you can give your baby than that?

Each sign you give your child is a precious gift, one that will be returned to you over and over. As your baby begins sharing his impressions of the world with you, you'll discover an exciting new place together, vibrant with color and imagination—in other words, the world as seen through his eyes.

No parent and child should miss out on this once-in-a-lifetime opportunity. However, signing with hearing babies is still a fairly new idea, and as of this writing, many people still haven't heard of it. Eventually, baby sign language classes will be as commonplace as childbirth classes, and many hospitals already do offer baby sign language as part of their women's health curriculum. Please help spread the word by sharing the gift of baby sign language with the other parents and caregivers in your life.

And now, let's really have some fun with what we've learned! Part IV will help you and your baby have a blast with your favorite signs.

part IV

signing
for fun

chapter 19

Signing
and Playing

Playtime provides a wonderful opportunity to make signing fun and engaging for you and your baby. You can integrate signs into just about any kind of playtime activity—the following are just a few suggestions. Enjoy!

- **Hide-and-Seek with Toys:** Place a toy partially under a blanket or behind your back. (Animal toys are good, as babies love animal signs!) Ask where the toy is, signing **WHERE,** and then ask, "Can you look for the **COW?**" or whatever it is you hid.

- **Hide-and-Seek with People:** Have one parent hide while baby and the other parent "seek." Sign and ask, **"WHERE** is **DADDY/MOMMY?"** Then add silliness and suspense by looking in ridiculous places, such as under rugs and in small drawers, before actually finding the person hiding.

- **Mirror Play:** This is a simple game that's very popular with babies. Sit in front of a mirror with your baby in your lap. Talk about yourself and your baby, your facial expressions and emotions, your body parts, your clothing, or his toys. You could sign **HAPPY, CRYING, I LOVE YOU,** or **"WHERE** is your **NOSE?"** Sign his body parts by circling them with your finger.

- **Guessing Game:** Sign and talk about pictures in a book and have baby find and point to them. Example: Sign "**WHERE** is the **ELEPHANT?**" then let baby find the picture of the **ELEPHANT** on the page.

- **Shoe Game:** You can play this game anywhere, anytime! Put your hands or fingers inside a pair of your baby's shoes and hit the shoes together. Sign **SHOES,** then show them **WALKING, RUNNING, JUMPING, DANCING**—making the signs after the shoes perform each action.

- **Simon Says:** This is a great toddler game. One parent can be "Simon" and say and sign commands such as "**WALK, RUN, JUMP, STOP,** or **GO,**" while the other parent and baby follow directions.

- **Doll Signs:** Sign to and about your child's favorite dolls or stuffed animals. This is a great way to make routine signs more motivating, since a child who doesn't show much interest in learning the **DIAPER CHANGE** sign might be engaged by performing this mundane task on his favorite teddy bear. Say and sign, "Let's **CHANGE** your **BEAR'S** diaper!"

- **Let's Pretend!:** Play "house," "store," or "fire sta-tion" with your child, and sign about the differ-ent things you're doing. A favorite game invented by my daughter was "buy new": We'd take shop-ping bags and "shop" for various items around the house, signing the items as we put them in the bag. We also bartered between our bags for each other's purchases.

- **Dress-Up Box:** Use signs to comment about the clothes, such as **HAT, COAT, SHOES,** or **BEAUTIFUL.**

Chapter 20

Storytime

igning along with books makes reading more fun and interactive for your baby and provides an opportunity to sign about things that are out of the realm of her day-to-day experiences. Combining pictures with vocabulary and signs reinforces new ideas for your baby and gives her a way to actively participate by commenting on the story and pictures.

When you read a story together, even when you're not signing, try to sit with your baby propped up across from you, "story-time-at-the-library" style. This will allow her to see your facial expressions and/or signs, and it also lets you see her reaction as you tell the story, which is a lot more fun than looking at the back of her head (even though the backs of babies' heads *are* very cute!).

When you read to your baby, remember that you don't have to read the entire story or even tell the *same* story that the author is telling. Babies have short attention spans, so pointing at the pictures (or letting your baby do the pointing) and talking about what you see generally works better than trying to follow the text word for word.

You can use signs with most picture books, but there are a few types that lend themselves especially well to signing and reading:

1. Books with one concept per page. Having only one concept per page makes it very clear to your baby what you're signing about. *Brown Bear, Brown Bear, What Do You See?* by Bill Martin, Jr., and Eric Carle is a great example of this type of book.

2. Books that repeat the same concept on each page. This type of book gives you the opportunity to reinforce one sign through repetition. *Goodnight Moon* and *The Runaway Bunny* by Margaret Wise Brown and Clement Hurd are good examples. Both books have bunnies on most pages, and *Goodnight Moon* has a mouse hiding on each page, too!

3. Vocabulary-building books with pictures of many objects on each page. These books are great for signed and verbal vocabulary building. You can also play a "let's-find" game by signing an object and asking your child to find it on the page. There are many of these books available, such as *Baby's Book of Animals* by Roger Priddy or *Richard Scarry's Best Word Book Ever* by Richard Scarry.

ASL books especially for children are also available. You can find them at your local library and at local and online bookstores. These books are really great because they often show pictures of children signing, are based on subjects of special interest to children, and include signs along with the pictures on each page. For a list of children's signing books, see the Resources section at the back of this book.

✖ ✖ ✖

You don't need to limit yourself to only reading children's books with your baby—any book or magazine with engaging pictures will do. Find pictures of babies and children in parenting magazines, food layouts in gourmet magazines, wildlife photos in *National Geographic* (but screen the content first for scary pictures!). Magazines for cat, dog, horse, boat, and car lovers are also great for showing many versions of the same thing. Are Chihuahuas and Great Danes really both dogs? Leafing through a copy of *Dog Fancy* magazine is a fun way to show just how many different kind of **DOGS** there are.

And reading isn't the only fun way to use your signs—there are plenty of nursery rhymes and songs that are fun to sign along with. Turn the page and you'll see what I mean!

chapter 21

Sing, Sign, and Rhyme!

Old McDonald

[Sign along with the animal name and sound!]

Old McDonald had a farm

E -I -E -I -O!

And on that farm he had a **COW**

E -I -E -I -O!

With a **MOO MOO** here

And a **MOO MOO** there

Here a **MOO**

There a **MOO**

Everywhere a **MOO MOO**

Old McDonald had a farm

E -I -E -I -O!

[Repeat with **HORSE, CHICKEN (BIRD), PIG, CAT, DOG**]

The Wheels on the Bus

The wheels on the **BUS (CAR)** go round and round
[circle fists round and round each other]
Round and round, round and round
The wheels on the **BUS** go round and round
All through the town

The **BABIES** on the **BUS** say, "I want **MILK,**
I want **MILK,** I want **MILK**"
The **BABIES** on the **BUS** say, "I want **MILK**"
All through the town

The **MOMMIES** on the **BUS** say, "**I LOVE YOU,**
I LOVE YOU, I LOVE YOU"
The **MOMMIES** on the **BUS** say, "**I LOVE YOU**"
All through the town

Are You Sleeping

Are you **SLEEPING,** are you **SLEEPING,**
BABY of mine, **BABY** of mine?
BABY likes to **SLEEP, BABY** likes to **SLEEP**
Let's **SLEEP MORE,** let's **SLEEP MORE**

Are you **EATING,** are you **EATING,**
BABY of mine, **BABY** of mine?
BABY likes to **EAT, BABY** likes to **EAT**
Let's **EAT MORE,** let's eat **MORE**

[Repeat with other verbs such as **WALKING,**
SINGING, DANCING, SWINGING, or **PLAYING**]

I've Got the Whole World

I've got a bouncy **BALL** in my hands
I've got a bouncy **BALL** in my hands
I've got a bouncy **BALL** in my hands
I've got a **BALL** in my hands

I've got a fluffy teddy **BEAR** in my hands
I've got a fluffy teddy **BEAR** in my hands
I've got a fluffy teddy **BEAR** in my hands
I've got a teddy **BEAR** in my hands

I've got a yummy **BANANA** in my hands
I've got a yummy **BANANA** in my hands
I've got a yummy **BANANA** in my hands
I've got a **BANANA** in my hands

I've got **MOMMY'S KEYS** in my hands
I've got **MOMMY'S KEYS** in my hands
I've got **MOMMY'S KEYS** in my hands
I've got her **KEYS** in my hands

191

Five Little Monkeys Jumping on the Bed

Five little **MONKEYS**

Jumping on the **BED**

One fell off and bumped his **HEAD** (**PAIN** at head)

MOMMY CALLED (telephone) the doctor

And the doctor said:

"**NO MORE MONKEYS**

JUMPING on the **BED!**"

Five Little Ducks

Five little **DUCKS** went out to **PLAY**
Over the hills and far away
MOMMY DUCK said, "**QUACK, QUACK, QUACK**"
And four little **DUCKS** came waddling back

Four little **DUCKS** went out to **PLAY**
Over the hills and far away
MOMMY DUCK said, "**QUACK, QUACK, QUACK**"
And three little **DUCKS** came waddling back
[Repeat with three, two, one, and no ducks]

MOMMY DUCK went far away
Looking for her **BABIES** who'd gone to **PLAY**
DADDY DUCK said, "**QUACK, QUACK, QUACK**"
And **MOMMY** and **BABIES** came waddling back

The More We Sign Together

The **MORE** we **SIGN** together, together, together
The **MORE** we **SIGN** together, the **HAPPIER** we'll be
For your **FRIENDS** are my **FRIENDS**
And my **FRIENDS** are your **FRIENDS**
The **MORE** we **SIGN** together, the **HAPPIER** we'll be
[Repeat with **SING, PLAY, HUG, DANCE,** and **JUMP**]

Three Nice Mice

Three nice **MICE,** three nice **MICE**
See how they **PLAY**, see how they **PLAY**
They're always polite when
they **NIBBLE (EAT)** their cheese
They always remember to say
THANK YOU and **PLEASE**
They cover their **NOSES** [finger circles nose]
whenever they **SNEEZE** [mime sneezing]
three nice **MICE**

If You're Happy and You Know It

If you're **HAPPY** and you know it, **CLAP** your hands
If you're **HAPPY** and you know it, **CLAP** your hands
If you're **HAPPY** and you know it
Then your **FACE** [index finger circles face]
will surely show it
If you're **HAPPY** and you know it, **CLAP** your hands
[Repeat with **BLOW A KISS,**
SHOUT HURRAY, and **JUMP FOR JOY**]

196

signing vocabulary

The following section contains 60 signs for use with babies and toddlers, listed alpha- betically. When you're ready for more signs or need one that isn't included here, you can refer to ASL dictionaries, which are available in the languages section at bookstores, online, and at your local library. Another wonderful resource is Michigan State University's ASL Browser Website, **www.commtechlab.msu.edu/sites/aslweb,** which shows a QuickTime video clip of the sign you're look- ing for. If you have Internet access, using this site is a great way to make sure that you've interpreted the signs you find in print correctly. With some signs, it can be difficult to determine the movement portion of the sign from a still picture (even if they have directional arrows), so watching a video of signs being produced can be very helpful.

In my descriptions of each sign, I sometimes refer to an *action hand* and a *base hand*. The action hand is the one that performs the movement portion of the sign, while the base hand is the one that remains stationary. The action hand should be your dominant hand—that is, the right hand for "righties" and the left hand for "lefties." With one-handed signs, "lefties" will sign with their left hand, while "righties" will sign with their right.

Airplane

The "Y" hand, with index finger
extended and palm down, moves up
and away from the body, representing
the wings and fuselage of an airplane
flying through the air.

Baby

One arm cradles the other
and rocks from side to side,
as if rocking a baby.

Ball

The curved hands, with fingers
spread, bounce toward each other,
as if holding a ball.

Banana

Go through the motions of peeling a banana: The extended index finger of the base hand represents the banana, while the fingertips of the action hand pull down the skin.

Bear

The two "claw hands" cross
across the chest and make
scratching motions, like a
bear scratching itself.

Bed

The tilted head is rested on the flat
palm, as if resting the head on a pillow.
(Can be used for **SLEEP** as well.)

Bird

The index finger and thumb
are held close to the mouth and
open and close like a bird's beak.

Blanket

The downturned hands
grasp and pull up an
imaginary blanket.

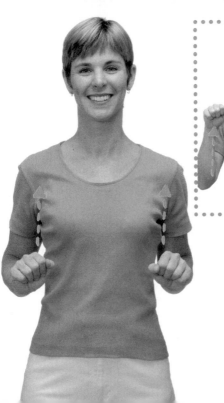

Car

Both hands move in opposite
arc motions, grasping an
imaginary steering wheel.

Cat

The thumb and index finger come together at the upper lip and move outward and away from the face, as if
sliding whiskers through the fingers.
(Can use one or both hands.)

Change

The two fists are held together, facing opposite directions, with knuckles touching. Both hands pivot in opposite directions, to change places.

Cold

The shoulders are hunched,
and the clenched hands shake
as if shivering with cold.

Cow

The thumb of the "Y" hand rests
on the temple and then moves
out and away in a slight curve,
indicating a cow's horn.
(Can use one or both hands.)

226

Cracker

The fist of the base hand is held
against the opposite shoulder,
as the action hand forms a fist
and strikes the elbow of the
base hand several times.

Daddy

The thumb of the sideways "five"
hand taps the middle of the forehead
several times. Fingertips may wiggle.

Dance

The first two fingers of the action
hand form an inverted "V" and swing
rhythmically back and forth over the
upturned palm of the base hand.

Dog

The hand pats the thigh and/or
snaps the fingers, as if calling a dog.

Drink

The signer tips an imaginary
glass to the open lips, as if drinking.

Duck

The action hand is held near the
mouth, facing out, while the first
two fingers open and close on top of
the thumb, indicating a duck's bill.

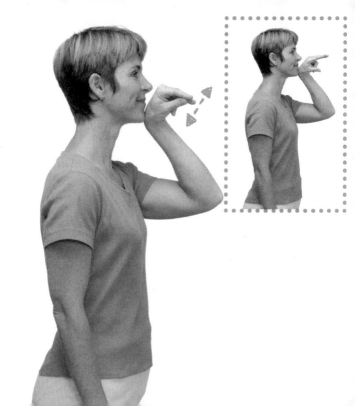

Eat

The fingers and thumb, held together
as if holding a small piece of food,
tap the mouth several times.

Elephant

Starting at the nose, the "C"
hand traces the shape of
an elephant's trunk.

242

Finished

Both "five" hands are held palms up,
then flip over in one swift motion.

Friend

The index fingers lock together,
then change positions and lock
the opposite way.

Gentle or Pet

One hand strokes the back
of the opposite hand.

Giraffe

The "C" hand starts at the
neck and moves up, tracing the
shape of the giraffe's neck.

Go

Both hands, with index fingers
extended, bend at the wrists and
point in the direction one is going.

Grandma

The "five" hand is held sideways
with the thumb touching the chin.
The hand then moves downward and
away in two arcs (similar to
MOMMY, but with two arcs, to
symbolize two generations).

Grandpa

The "five" hand is held sideways, with
the thumb touching the forehead.
The hand then moves downward and
away in two arcs (similar to
DADDY, but with two arcs, to
symbolize two generations).

256

Happy

The flat hand pats the chest
repeatedly with an upward stroking
movement, representing happy
feelings bubbling up.

Help

The action hand, formed into a fist, is placed on top of the flat base hand. Both rise up together as if the flat hand is helping to lift the fist.

Non-ASL version, as recommended for very young children by Joseph Garcia in *SIGN with your BABY:* Both flat hands pat the chest.

Non-ASL Version

Horse

The thumb touches the temple, while
the extended first two fingers flap
up and down together, like a horse's
ear. (Can use one or both hands.)

Hot

The signer holds the hand like
a claw, palm facing the mouth,
then drops the palm downwards
as if spitting out hot food and
throwing it on the floor.

I Love You

I **LOVE YOU** can be signed as three separate signs, or by using one single gesture.

I: Index finger points to self.
LOVE: Fists cross over the chest at wrists.
YOU: Index finger points to other person.

I LOVE YOU: The "Y" hand is held up with the index finger extended.

I LOVE YOU

I

LOVE

YOU

Jump

The first two fingers of the
action hand form an inverted "V"
on the palm of the base hand.
The action hand springs up and
down, representing legs jumping.

Keys

The index finger of the action hand
bends at the knuckle and turns in the
sideways palm of the base hand,
representing a key turning in a lock.

Milk

The sideways-held fist is
opened and closed several times,
as if milking a cow.

Mommy

The thumb of the sideways "five" hand taps the chin several times. Fingertips may wiggle.

Monkey

The hands scratch up and down on the sides, imitating a monkey.

More

The thumbs and fingertips of each hand are held together, and the fingertips of both hands tap together several times. Represents gathering more things together.

Mouse

The fist is held in front of the chin as
the extended index finger brushes
across the nose several times,
indicating a mouse's twitching nose.

Music

The action hand, held on its side,
moves rhythmically back and forth
over the forearm, which is held in
front of the chest.

No

The first two fingers close down on the thumb. This is a variation of the finger spelling of "O."

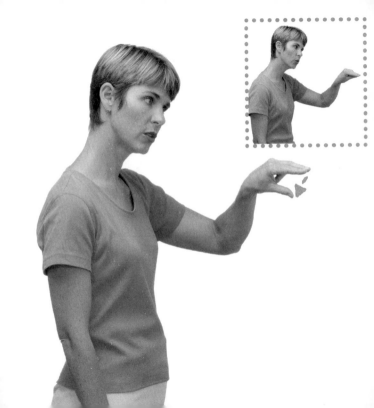

Pain

The two index fingers tap together several times at the location of the pain. The face should show a pained expression.

EARACHE

STOMACHACHE

Pig

The hand flaps up and down
underneath the chin, representing
food dripping from the mouth of
a pig. The sign for **DIRTY** is the
same, but with fingers wiggling
instead of the hand flapping.

Play

The "Y" hands are shaken,
pivoting at the wrists, representing
the shaking of a tambourine.

Please

The open palm touches the chest
and moves in a circular motion.

Scared

The fists face each other,
then suddenly move together with
palms opening and fingers shaking.
A startled expression on the
face is important.

Share

The little finger of the side-facing
action hand brushes back and forth
along the index finger of the sideways base hand, which has its thumb
extended. (Represents dividing
things up to be shared.)

Shoes

The thumb-sides of the fists
tap together, representing
someone clicking the heels
of their shoes together.

Sign

The index fingers are extended
upward and move in alternating
circles, representing the motion of
the hands when a person is signing.

Sit

The first two fingers of one
hand "sit" on the first two fingers
of the opposite hand, representing
legs sitting on a bench.

Sorry

The fist moves in a circular
motion on the chest.

Stop

The edge of one hand comes
down on the palm of the other,
representing something coming
to a quick stop. (A guillotine,
perhaps? After all, American Sign
Language *is* very closely related
to French Sign Language.)

306

Swing

The first two fingers of one hand
form an inverted "V" and bend to sit
on the first two fingers of the opposite hand. Both move back and forth
in an arc, like a person on a swing.

Telephone

The Y" hand is held to
the side of the head,
representing a telephone.

Thank You and You're Welcome

The fingertips of the flat hand
touch the lips and then move out
and down toward the person
being thanked, representing nice
words coming from the mouth.

Tiger

The bent fingers of both hands
are pulled across the face,
representing a tiger's stripes.

Walk

The downturned palms move
alternately toward and away
from the chest, representing
the movement of walking feet.

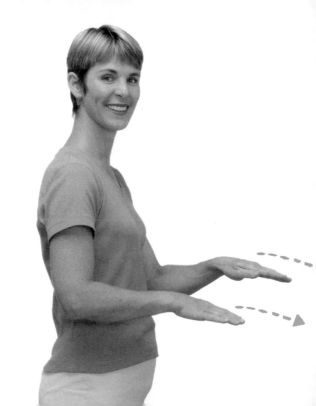

Water

The index, middle, and ring fingers
are extended to form a "W" hand.
The "W" taps the chin twice.

Where

The hand, with index finger
extended, waves from side to
side, describing a small arc.

resources

Baby Sign Language Books

Sign with your Baby Complete Learning Kit, by Joseph Garcia (North-light Communications, Seattle, WA, 1999). This kit includes the book *Sign with your Baby* (which includes 145 ASL signs), an instructional video, and a laminated reference chart. The components of the kit can also be purchased separately. Please visit **www.sign2me.com.**

Baby Signs: How to Talk to Your Baby Before Your Baby Can Talk, by Linda Acredolo, Ph.D., and Susan Goodwyn, Ph.D., with Douglas Abrams ("McGraw-Hill/Contemporary Books, Columbus, OH, 2002). Drs. Acredolo and Goodwyn conducted a long-term study on using sign-ing with hearing babies, funded by the National Institutes of Health and Human Development. This book contains their findings, develop-mental information, strategies, and activities. There's only one drawback: Many of the signs included are not actual ASL signs.

Dancing with Words: Signing for Hearing Children's Literacy, by Marilyn Daniels (Bergin & Garvey, Westport, CT, 2000). This book focuses on how signing with children enhances literacy and reading skills.

ASL Dictionaries

Signs for Me: Basic Sign Vocabulary for Children, Parents, and Teachers, by Ben Bahan and Joe Dannis (DawnSignPress, San Diego, CA, 1990). This book of kid-friendly signs is organized grammatically and thematically. The signers in the pictures are children, and the large pictures are suitable for coloring.

Random House Webster's American Sign Language Dictionary, by Elaine Costello (Random House, New York, NY, 1999). Available in full, concise, and pocket versions. The pocket version is the best because of its tiny size and *plastic cover!* Don't leave home without it!

American Sign Language Dictionary, by Martin L.A. Sternberg (Harper-Collins, New York, NY, 1998). Available in full or concise versions.

Children's Books
(Amazon.com has the widest selection)

Animal Signs: A First Book of Sign Language, by Debby Slier (Gallaudet University Press, Washington, D.C., 1995). These board books contain illustrations and corresponding signs.

Baby's First Signs and *More Baby's First Signs,* by Kim Votry and Kurt Waller (Gallaudet University Press, Washington, D.C., 2001). These are beautiful board books!

Word Signs: A First Book of Sign Language, by Debby Slier (Gallaudet University Press, Washington, D.C., 1995). This board book contains object photos and corresponding signs.

Opposites: A Beginner's Book of Signs and *Happy Birthday: A Beginner's Book of Signs,* by Angela Bednarczyk, et al. (Star Bright Books, Long Island City, NY, 1997). This board book contains object photos and corresponding signs.

My First Book of Sign Language, by Joan Holub (Troll Assoc., Memphis, TN, 1998).

Simple Signs, by Cindy Wheeler (Puffin, London, England, 1997).

You Can Learn Sign Language!: More Than 300 Words in Pictures, by Jackie Kramer, et al. (Troll Assoc., Memphis, TN, 2000).

An Alphabet of Animal Signs, by S. Harold Collins, et al. (Garlic Press, Eugene OR, 2001). Contains an animal sign for each letter of the alphabet.

Pets, Animals & Creatures, by Jane Phillips, et al. (Garlic Press, Eugene, OR, 2001). Photos and signs for 77 pets, farm animals, and wild animals. Garlic Press has many other wonderful signing books for children! Check out **www.garlicpress.com.**

My First Baby Signs; Baby Signs for Mealtime; Baby Signs for Animals; and *Baby Signs for Bedtime,* by Linda Acredolo, et al. (HarperFestival, New York, NY, 2002). These board books feature cute signing baby photos (but they're not all ASL signs).

Videos

The Treasure Chest, by Wide-Eyed Learning (Portland, OR, and Denver, CO, 2003). Engaging and educational video for children and adults. Please visit **www.wideeyedlearning.com.**

Sign with your Baby, by Northlight Communications (Seattle, WA, 1999). Instructional video for adults.

Sign Songs, by Education 2000 (1998). Instructional video featuring favorite children's songs.

Blues Clues: All Kinds of Signs, by Paramount Studios (Hollywood, CA, 2001).

Sign-Me-a-Story, by Sony Wonder (1987).

Talking Hands: A Sign Language Video for Children, by Small Fry Productions (Alpharetta, GA, 2001).

Baby See 'N Sign: Volume 1, by Kronz Kidz Productions (Creswell, OR, 2001). Excellent learning video with more than 60 signs for babies and toddlers.

Baby See 'N Sign: Volume 2, by Kronz Kidz Productions (Creswell, OR, 2003). Excellent learning video with more than *100* signs for babies and toddlers, including a bonus signing section on manners!

Signing Time: Volumes 1, 2, and *3* (also music CD), by Two Little Hands Productions (Draper, UT, 2002). A must-have! Features a deaf child and her younger hearing cousin.

Music

Pick Me Up! by Northlight Communications (Seattle, WA, 2003). Music CD and hardcover activity guide with tear-resistant pages. Wonderful children's music that won't grate on your nerves, in musical styles like Sinatra, The Beach Boys, Elvis, and more. Available at **www.sign2me.com.**

Baby Sign Language Workshops Signing Songs CD, Mylaboo Music (San Rafael, CA, 2004). Originals and children's favorites from our signing classes. Available at **www.babysignlanguageworkshops.com.**

Other Media

Reminder Series Poster/Placemats by Northlight Communications (Seattle, WA, 2002). Laminated posters in eight themes. Each poster presents concepts in ASL, English, and Spanish and are the perfect size for placemats or posting on walls. Available at **www.sign2me.com**.

endnotes

Chapter 3
1. *Baby Signs,* Linda Acredolo, Ph.D., and Susan Goodwyn, Ph.D.

Chapter 4
1. *Baby Signs,* Linda Acredolo, Ph.D., and Susan Goodwyn, Ph.D.
2. *Save Your Baby: Throw Out Your Equipment,* Laura Sobell.

Chapter 7
1. *Signing Smart Beginner Curriculum,* Michelle Anthony, M.A., Ph.D., and Reyna Lindert, Ph.D.

Chapter 9
1. *Sign with your Baby,* Joseph Garcia.
2. "Making Every Sign Count," Patricia Spencer, Ph.D., *Perspectives in Education and Deafness,* Vol. 17, #2.

Chapter 16
1. *Sign with your Baby:* **www.sign2me.com** or 877-744-6263.
2. Ibid.

about the author

Monta Briant, a native of San Francisco, California; and her husband, Paul, of Cape Town, South Africa, began signing with their daughter, Sirena, when she was six months old. The family eventually learned hundreds of signs together. Monta was so moved by the experience of being able to communicate effectively with her then-preverbal daughter that she found herself telling anyone pushing a stroller about baby sign language.

In 2001, Monta, a former professional yacht captain, decided to make a permanent career change that would enable her to stay home with Sirena—she founded Baby Sign Language Workshops. An enthusiastic speaker and self-proclaimed "baby sign language evangelist," Monta teaches workshops and signing classes throughout San Diego County and is also available for speaking engagements. Baby Sign Language Workshops classes have been the subject of feature stories in the *San Diego Union-Tribune* and on *Fox 6 News* in San Diego.

Monta is a member of SIGN *with your* BABY™ Presenters Network, and can be reached at **Monta@babysignlanguage.net.** For class schedules and other information, please visit **www.babysignlanguage.net.**

We hope you enjoyed this Hay House Lifestyles book. If you would like to receive a free catalog featuring additional Hay House books and products, or if you would like information about the Hay Foundation, please contact:

Hay House, Inc.
P.O. Box 5100
Carlsbad, CA 92018-5100

(760) 431-7695 or **(800) 654-5126**
(760) 431-6948 (fax) or **(800) 650-5115 (fax)**
www.hayhouse.com

Published and distributed in Australia by:
Hay House Australia, Ltd. • 18/36 Ralph St. • Alexandria NSW 2015 •
Phone: 612-9669-4299 • *Fax:* 612-9669-4144 • www.hayhouse.com.au

Published and distributed in the United Kingdom by:
Hay House UK, Ltd. • Unit 62, Canalot Studios •
222 Kensal Rd., London W10 5BN • *Phone:* 44-20-8962-1230 •
*Fax:*44-020-8962-1239 • www.hayhouse.co.uk

Published and distributed in the Republic of South Africa by:
Hay House SA (Pty), Ltd., P.O. Box 990, Witkoppen 2068 •
Phone/Fax: 2711-7012233 • orders@psdprom.co.za

Distributed in Canada by:
Raincoast • 9050 Shaughnessy St., Vancouver, B.C. V6P 6E5 •
Phone: (604) 323-7100 • *Fax:* (604) 323-2600